"Rye. You are insanely gifted" —
Vicky Phelan on Vicky In The Flat

"For me the work he is producing is so moving and in my opinion more powerful and possibly more important than the work he was tasked with initially."
— artist Alan Flannery

"Your words got us through lockdown/COVID, thank you"
— Valerie Leahy

"We should be naming pies, parks and much more after him, capturing and captivating us."
— Dee Hart

"I recall Pat Ingoldsby making me smile the way Rye Aker makes me smile."
— Patrick Denny

"You have woven a blanket of words of comfort and gratitude on the nation's behalf."
— Gay Murphy

Definitely a highlight of 2020 and brought many smiles
Míle buíochas, Rye Aker, you brightened up a strange year and Galway 2020 programme.
— Orla Flynn, GMIT

Hundred Akers

To Be Among

The Galway Collection Vol II

Rye Aker

CONTENTS

Galway and Rye

In the Spring of 2019, it was decided that I would come to Ireland to try to capture in verse the European Capital of Culture status of the city of Galway and its surrounds. I had been to Ireland many times before as a backpacking student, and the prospect excited me.

But like the best documentary projects, it snowballed into something else. I have come here and made friends, but the year was waylaid by unbelievable natural disasters. Storms that lashed the west coast; waves that upturned cars; floods that made hard farmers cry and a virus that shut down the earth.

In my first collection of poetry from Galway called A Penance of Sundays, I recalled a year in which I had experienced a piece of Galway pre Covid, and was then able to compare the two. In this collection, my poems are my complete immersion into an Ireland in lockdown, experiencing the ups and downs along with the rest of the population, sharing tough times, funny times and strange times with a people who are very close to my heart.

The main reason I have come here has been sadly shattered by the Covid-19, but this has not deterred me from portraying this beautiful place in words and common expression. I have amassed maybe five thousand expressions from friends, and from research and I hope to use many of these in my work.

None of this has been like I thought it would be, but I have to say that this has been the best year of my life. I have left my mobile cellphone back in Holland. I check Twitter messages just every week or so in my splendid semi-isolation. I have been interviewed for some newspapers and radio, but I wish to keep myself back for my first love, my words. So please forget about me the person and just drink the words.

I have offered my services with no fee to many charities and I remain willing to do what I can to use my words to help those people who are at this very moment helping someone else. Life is short, my friends. If my words can bring a laugh or a moment of reflection, I am glad to do so. If I can raise funds or make a highlight of the work these people do, please get in touch and I will be of service.

I thank my friends in Galway who are helping me with advice and guidance, and who laugh at my antics. To those who have cars and bicycles and help deliver my books to shops and to places I cannot get to. To James and Declan and Terry and Maureen and Dirk and Seamus and Bernie and Siobhan. To everyone in Galway 2020 and in the charities I worked with. To the team at AIB's The Toughest and their charities, whom I was only too glad to help, a thank you. To Vicky Phelan, my love and virtual energy.

I hope you all enjoy this collection of poetry written between August 2020 and March 2021. Maybe in time, these words might not have the meaning they possessed when I wrote them, and for me that is good. They are a snapshot in a moment when everything was so strange. I thank you for buying this book, for putting food in my fridge, and I look forward to even more poems as our world rights itself after its biggest shock ever.

My friends, I love you all. Love each other and see you on the far side of this.

Rye Aker, Galway 2021 — @RyeAker

Front cover design and illustrations throughout by Dirk de Vries
Layout: Teri de Leeuw

First Edition — 2021

During the lockdown, there was political scandal in Ireland when a politicians' golf society held a dinner in a Connemara hotel, in breach of the recommended guidelines. It led to resignations but before that, there was a flurry of apologies, so I penned this poem.

Sorry

I'm sorry if what I did upset you in any way...
and if it didn't, I'm not.

I'm sorry the livestream froze on your granny's Mass
because the proper broadband
never came up the road
her hearse bounced down.

I'm sorry that you pulled back the partition on
our arrogance and self importance, saw us
intellectually naked with the tide out.
Swapping tales of when we really mattered.

I'm sorry you don't think those supposed to
advocate for you can get together in one room
and not judge something is wrong.

I'm sorry that confirmations and weddings
are shallow sorrowful affairs with dressed up aunties
holding envelopes in the carpark
and recorded hymns echoing
over every empty varnished pew.

But most of all, I'm sorry for taking a bit of
the gloss off all of us.
For ruining our buzz.
For having golfgate emboldened
in every Boolean search of our life.
Forever.

I'm sorry.

Really?

Arra, sorry me hole.

I was honoured to be asked to write the official poem for AIB's
The Toughest campaign, to pay tribute to the great work that GAA club
members did in communities up and down the country.

All Togged Out

Who knew in December's sheds steeped in rich scents
of sweat and spits and winter cream and wet socks
that muscles honed and shaped to snatch a sliotar
would reach instead for shelves of tins and banks of turf?

That glistening calves primed for racing towards the H at the town end
would stretch up crooked paths where grateful smiles through net curtains
took the ham and bread and Bag for Life of kind words from
those with the village flag on their chests and in their hearts.

Who knew that grass that snuggled 'neath the spring frost
would not get a decent haircut til summer; that its lengthy blades
would wrap the hefty padlock and tell the world the pitch was closed.
A flag of tricoloured dandelions wrapping silent fields in a country fallen
quiet.

They are giants who never knew the best decision they'd make all year
would not be to pass or shoot, but to choose the right cat food
for the trembling hands. Those for whom they fight and catch
and pull and kick. Those who make up their place.

When it mattered, the Tuatha de Danann rose two-handed
against the wirey Formorian that crept through our streets.
They stepped over that white line, and softened the fear,
shattering an invisibility into which their years had lured them.

Without the summer sounds of the Micheals crackling through earphones
in the hairy ears of the long departed in the lonely bedsits of Cricklewood,
a sporting army swam in a sea of soundness.
Athletes hewed from the toughest stone ensured not one was left behind.

All togged out for the panel of getting on withgetting on with it.
Not a cow left unmilked or a child left bored.
Now the thud of boot on ball ringing
over the village
is a sonic reminder that when
it mattered,
everyone mattered.

On the evening that Kamala Harris was named on the Democratic ticket, a meteorite shower lit up the skies, as if the planets gave their blessing in the interest of nature.

The Night Joe Named Kamala

The night Joe named Kamala,
the planets sent their rocks
of approval lashing our atmosphere
like lockdown hurlers mad for wall
in an echoing ball alley.
While yer man finished his
pint of PhishFood and twiddled thumbs
to tweet if her hands were as big as his,
the skies celebrated a reprieve
from the world of crazy.
To show that in the dark night
there is a hope that we can reset
the world to make it right.
To return the fools to the hill.
To learn the lesson that we
Can never take life for granted again.

I always feel that the lack of leadership in the United States prolonged the battle against Covid 19. Then it emerged that the President was in possession of the full facts and that he had played down the significance.

Playing It Down

When the one book on your shelf
hasn't even been fully coloured in.
When your truth fails the
test under the Trade Description Act.
When you forego Deep Throat from All The President's Men
for a screenshot from Debbie Does Dallas.
When you see your reflection in the spoon scooping
out the pint of cherry vanilla as you stomp
the corridors in your MAGA underpants.
When you peer through the gaps,
see the dark clouds over Lafayette Square
And know that playing it down to keep your numbers up
is as close to playing God as makes no difference.
When you kill the belief that everyone has
in whom they should believe.
You have trampled the saplings of facts
on the darkened forest floor.

Then you know that maybe you're not as clever
as you thought you are, but are as clever
as we thought you are. That at a time when
the world needed a leader more than ever,
you chose to be a slave to those to whom
you were beholden because You Are Who You Are
And therefore incapable of anything better.

The world does not have a vote
in your most important pageant.
But every child born this night
Across the globe has a stake.

In 1982, as a 19-year-old, I had a summer job at the Barcelona Nou Camp stadium for the summer's World Cup. I sold ice-cream and snacks and pop, just twenty metres from where a young Diego Maradona warmed up before the opening game against Belgium. I was saddened to hear of his death in 2020.

No 10

For Diego

Almost four decades back
on a sunny Spanish evening,
I trekked up and down steps.
A leather bag of snacks
hanging off my chest
in the Camp Nou.
Warm shadows beating
on a global festival about to begin.
Five years and a world between us.
You serving up wonder.
Me serving up snacks and drinks.
You arrived as a prince
and stretched yourself before me
My heart beat strong to be in your space
You took warmup corners, 50 metres from me
Each one drilled along that line.
You hit that post each time.
Such straight shots, such magic.
You lost that night in a match
that gave us the iconic shot
of you versus six. And
I worked in bars that summer
And went home in the Fall.
You went home just weeks later

And now you have passed
after a life of turbulence waves,
I see goals and shots and tearful fans.
of Maracana and San Paolo.
Yet I never forget that evening
when for you and I,
two young men,
the world seemed
wondrous,
stretched out before us.

Oh, the consternation there was when the letter writers to the Times got stuffy about the queues of ordinary people outside Penneys when it reopened after lockdown.

Knicker aggro ah

They'd penned their letters to
The Irish Times before the first
crotchless knicker was scanned
through the Tuesday till at Penney's.
"Am I the only one..." they started
with the Dalkey wind blowing through
their window "to think it reckless
that these...these... people
should risk Our Lives by gathering
in the wee small hours of the morning
to buy their garish pinks and yellows
And push ups and shove downs.
And then to boast about it
on the streets where we ourselves,
Our people, will wait politely in line
for the latest Misa dress and tickets
For La Rigoletto, while Himself
tee-ed off as the sun rose.

On Moscow's streets, once
you saw a queue you joined it.
Now you rush to print the
tut tuts of your missing out
to a waiting world of your
peers without empathy.

Has anyone given a thought to our sleeves? Once the receptors of the contents of noses and mouths, now surpassed by the elbows in this new normal.

Snot fair

Think of the sleeves of Ireland
this winter; visited upon them
the grossest of indignities.
Their partners just up a bit
faring not much better.
Once they had a job to do.
To hold an elbow shape;
The curve of a limb,
a catwalk for the strutting sensuosity
at the juncture of muscle
with that enabler of dexterity,
Now those protectors
of corners and wrists feel sodden.
Never more than an itch away
from a blast of nose;
a full throat of cough.
They forego their stylish
roles for the slopping out
of the head, denied privileges.
Their world changed forever.
When for them, will
there be a new normal?
When Paddy goes back to
sneezing into his hand;
A thumb on one nostril
while he evacuates the other.
They have done their bit
for their country, yet will they
be named in a new year's honour's list.
Will they fuck?

Many people gasped when An Taoiseach said in the Dáil that the bank bailout had never happened.

On mature recollection

Ray Houghton never got
that goal against England.
Never. Didn't get near it.
Own goal it was, said the
country's leader when
scoring his own.

Who is this Johnny Logan lad ye say
won the Eurovision twice?
Twice. Twice, sure now
we can't even get out
of our own country.
Don't be talking rubbish.
Ráiméis. Never happened.

When the opposition
looked longingly at
the empty spaces 'neath
their Christmas tree,
didn't the Government
that keeps on giving
wrap one up for them.

With a big bow. A Táin Bó
swiping flies with a
festive tail of the unexpected
Nudging a bale out of the
barns of rewritten history.

In Ireland we felt a sense of duty when Vicky Phelan told the nation she was going to America on her own, to receive treatment. So I conceived the idea of us all being her flatmates. This work received one million views on social media.

Vicky in the flat

The new girl moved in next door. From Ireland.
And four million Irish flatmates with her, with their arragh go on
at the end of each day. Asking her 'what's the craic?'
And did ya get milk on the way back, and the four million and one of ye
fighting over the remote control to watch
500 mad channels in a daft country offering you everything
From condos in Orlando to stopping the steal.

This new girl from Ireland, she's beautiful and inspirational
and the flatmates love her, because they know
that on the day when history sits down to write its wrongs
and when all of us who read this will look up at Irish sunlight
streaming down through the hollowed stems of dandelions,
there will be people who will live because Vicky does.

These flatmates know their daughters and mothers
and sisters and aunts won't be fobbed off anymore
because of what the new girl from Ireland has done for them.
Making a throne of the best seat in the room.
they'll make the tay for Vicky. Sitting her down
rubbing her feet and filling her in with the goss of the day
'tween painting her toenails and admiring the Duke from Bridgerton.
So that when they've stopped their fussing, she's fit for the leaba
And the sleep of sleeps before the next day.

And when she sleeps, they'll stand guard in the kitchen
and whisper softly over steaming cups of hot chocolate, their belief
that when musty shadows threw shades of grey through the
net curtains of the squinting windows, her hand drew back,
let flood in the brightness of reality, set free
the chained mentions of the unmentionables.
A Markiewicz for the new time.
A woman who stood up for the nation
that had harmed her and many others.
And made it a better place.
When Ireland marks 200 years of wrestled freedom,
her name will be tapped into the clean stone
of walls to shield the work of those who changed it.

And in the morning, the flatmates will guide her through leafy streets of Maryland.
She'll feel their breath when she needs it most and do
this every day until they guide her back home again through duty free
and the flight from Gate Four, returning this national asset to this shore
where the rest of us can mind her once again.

Historically, we mistakenly make the assumption that the faith of the lad who stands in the porch at Mass is less than that of the person in the front row. But it is not. Last summer when people were assigned seats at worship, I wondered what would happen to him.

The Lad At The Back Of The Church

The Lad At The Back Of The Church is lost,
confused, suddenly Godless. He's been slippin'
in after the First Reading since Gerd Muller was in his prime.
Slipping out after Communion to get the Sunday World
and a head start on the chops, the peas, and the jelly
Telling the Mother who said the Last Mass
and what he was on about and who he saw.

The Lad At The Back Of The Church
pretended to pray with his porch pilgrims.
Nodded at each other. Took a knee when he had to.
Peered through the misty glass up the aisle
at the silent hum of the thronged.
Shuffled on one foot, scratching themselves
All gasping for a fag, a Sweet Afton
itching in his pocket for a meeting
with Maguire and Patterson

The Lad At The Back Of The Church
used to clear his throat with a Sunday morning
spit out past the font into the yard
Smile at the Holy Joes in the first seats
all hoping that nearer my God to thee
was an instruction of an usher from beyond.
He wondered if they were holier than himself
or was their journey here every weekend
along a smoother path from self righteousness.

The Lad At The Back Of The Church is confused.
Face half covered, sparkling eyes morse coding a message to life.
Porch is empty save for masked stewards.
Now the smell of booze comes from the hand sanitiser.
Nobody would dare light up lest
the church would blow To Kingdom Come.
Now they take his name and number, and guide him shyly to
a front row where he hadn't sat since the Mother died.
Up here, nodding to himself, twitching at the
thought of all the heads behind looking at his.

The Lad At The Back Of The Church can't
be doing with all this fussing, but many of the lads
he prayed and smoked with have come down

that aisle on their backs, so he needs credit
because everyone is dying these days.
Some sort of cashing out for all the porch masses
he has taken in when it would have been easier
to lie in a pool of porter on a Sunday morning.
So now, he sits in the car, turns the dial to the padre,
nods to himself and vapes.

When Tanáiste Leo Varadkar and Chief Medical Officer Tony Holohan had a difference of opinion before Christmas, we yearned for the days they were a double act.

When love breaks down

It's different now.
Time has changed them.
The Cagney and Lacey
of the summertime chats
on the steps of some official place
chosen to hear the teatime roll-call
of the dead. They've stropped and strutted.
Absence made the heart wander.
You never wrote, you never called
and then they storm back into our lives
with this.

Sunday nights are for finding out
you've no yoghurt for the school lunch.
For ironing the cleanest dirty school shirt.
For finding deep in the bag,
the note sent home on a Thursday
about some event on a Saturday.

Sunday nights are not for whispered sweet
nothings to a hack's ear that what you want
is more than you ever said you wished for.
And more than I or my new love could ever give.

So the sound of a bus approaching is too
inviting. Like Aesop's scorpion
pretending to push the walk button at the pedestrian crossing,
the first shots fired in a war where the victor is determined
by the beeping cacophony of a dark ward in a macabre
Halloween sacrifice of the rights and wrongs.

The people of Yeats' Sligo were aghast when it was suggested that slow customer service at eir was in some way attributable to the fact that they were not very good at it.

An Irish Eir-man foresees his death

An Irish Eir-man foresees his death.
Lost in the cloud, momentarily
Uttering 'please hold because your call
Is so important to us.' Forgive us,
Do not cast a cold eye on Benjamin Bulben.
And the others who might be allegedly
shit at customer service.
Many horsemen pass by
While you wait and wait.
Enjoy the muzak and note:
"Please do not swear.
You are live at Mullaghmore."
Your call might be recorded
and used for training porpoises, lest
Fungi swims in at Rosses Point
to try his hand in the call centre.
I will eir-rise now and go to a caller
from Inisfree. And in a small cabin built
there for working from home,
I meet them at close of day.
Coming with vivid faces stunned,
from their headsets. Transformed.
Utterly, their terrible beauty.
Born.
This is no job for old men
Or young women, hanging here like Blondie
on the telephone, too long the sacrifice
making a stone of my heart.
No time for fumbling in a greasy till
Hold your ire, your fire at me because
the reason you are waiting is because of here.
There is no history of Please Hold
in the place that gave us Yeats.
I know you did not mean to hurt us
when you said we were not good.
I implore you not to rush to judge us.
I have spread my dreams under your feet;
Tread softly because you tread on my dreams.
Romantic Ireland might be dead and gone
But please hold Mr O'Leary, your call
Is important to us.

Most years, we enjoy the changing of the season and its implication for a Sunday morning 'lie-in' but this year when we had enough free time, it meant nothing to us.

The extra hour in bed

In a year that can't end soon enough,
what would I be doing with
an extra hour of anything.
Nothing to wait up for.
Nothing to get up for.

I don't want the day to feel longer
or the dawn to come sooner
or there to be any more value
in a time that nobody wants
elongated.

There's no Mass to be late for.
No hungover stubble to scrape away.
No need for an extra hour
to clean a house
to which nobody will come.

You can hide your lie-in eyes
As there's no reminding call
from the Mother who doesn't
trust Steve Jobs to change your clocks.

Maybe in the late Spring or Fall,
I will forfeit the hour forward.
In a well world again,
I will embrace every
moment.
Every hour.
Backwards
or
forwards.

There have been so many sad landmarks in Ireland in 2020, but the moment that the country hit 4,000 deaths from Covid-19 was particularly poignant.

Four thousand gone

There's a lot of bread
left unbuttered;
A lot of front rooms
wallpapered in red and gold
like the Gaiety.
Never to be seen on nights
when the front and back doors
Are thrown open for in and out
To blow the gust of grief through
a bungalow built from a plan in a book.

A typed condolence on RIP.ie
might let the people know
you're sorry for their troubles, but
it also shows why woodwork
was your strongest subject at school.
It's no handshake,
No hug, no grasp of the sweated hand
with palms soaked by the collective
damp of people from your place.
Those who know your pain.

Too many families have felt
the gale of an empty graveyard.
No outer ring of neighbours
to save them from a weather
that doesn't recognise death.
Left to fill the days after
to listen to the tick and the tock
on a mantelpiece over an empty grate
in the devastating silence
of a country thrown quiet.

Four thousand gone.
The size of
ten Late Late Shows
with a death
for everyone
In the audience.

The fallout from the Golfgate saga continued throughout the year and the travails of the Supreme Court judge rumbled out in the news for many many weeks.

Bench marks

When the waiter asked the Judge if it'd be the Salmon or the lamb
he'd be having and
If he wanted the sauce on the side, before signing off with
'no further questions, your honour,'
nobody knew that it would be the racks of Minister on a leafy
bed of Commissioner
that would soon festoon that ju-Dish-ery in the shadow of the Twelve Pins.

So the Judge in his judgement and who normally loved the news
but didn't have the radio on those days decided to say sorry anyway
for something or other
or in that great line 'for any offence that might have been caused'
as if it is our fault for being offended.
But when the Top Judge asked the Second Judge to talk to
the Lamb Judge, the Lamb Judge told the Second Judge that it was
much ado about nothing
That twasn't his fault at all and that he barely touched the dinner
and in his judgement didn't know there were two halves to the room
and had no idea why the boxes of George Foreman grills and toasters
were going through a gap in the wall.

But when the Gaggle of Judges heard that the Second Judge
had given the First Judge three Hail Mary's and an
Our Father before sending him on his way, the gaggle fired
up the cauldron and asked to meet the Lamb Judge
to give him a piece of their considered judgement, but the
Lamb Judge had watched enough of Tom and Jerry when
studying at Kings Inns to know when not to run into a trap,
so showed clever judgement to be not judged by the gaggle of judges

But the Top Judge felt that what the Second Judge had decided
wasn't far enough, in his judgement, so he told the Lamb Judge
that in the line of Jim Reeve, he'd have to go.
That there'd be no wolf in judge's clothing and that
'twasn't for the balls o' mash he'd be going,
but the judgement shown by the Lamb Judge, said the Top Judge.

But the Judge who ordered the lamb was not going to be
sacrificial and said he'd give up sweets for lent, do a 48-hour fast
for Concern, pack bags at his local SuperValu
if he could just pease please please hold onto the gig.
He'd even volunteer to clean the shit out of the cuckoo clock
in the Top Judge's chambers at the Four Courts.
Until February.

Because in his Judgement, all those who walked the plank for
'atin Lamb in the middle of a Pandemic would hang onto their earnings,
that they'd just lost their privileges not their entire livelihood.
And that in his judgement, the judgement of the other Judge
And the other Judges the Top Judge talked to was ill-judged.

Now the Top Judge who ignored the report of the Second Judge
Into the Lamb Judge doesn't want to misjudge it, so they've rolled
Up all of those balls of mash, and dropkicked them across the Liffey
To let the others sort it out.

I was very annoyed when hundreds of students partied together at the Spanish Arch at the start of the semester. Perhaps, I was annoyed too much? In hindsight, maybe I was. Or was I?

Hope you enjoyed your beer

I hope you enjoyed your beer,
flowing hitting that spot like when
they yank back your throat
to prepare you for the ventilator.

I hope you enjoyed your piss
on the steps of the church or
in the garden of the widow
whose husband planted flowers
and prayed for rain before the cat
claws were scraped across his lungs
and he thrust out a cooling hand
that would not be clasped.

I hope you enjoyed your songs
of fuck you to the nurses with
elastic marks eaten into their faces
as they stripped in dark dawn sheds with
cheap bin bags to hold the clothes
stinking of that night's death, dripping
of the dappled moisture of fading life.

I hope you are not just scholars
lost on a sea of exuberance
allowed the youth, although
who among you is too young
not to know the breadth
of what you were asked not to do?

I hope your disdain of this place
melts to a shielded shame. Postpone
your freedom dance until the moon
clouds roll away and the joy of a few
cans reflect the rising sun on a new time.

Back in the summer when we had just 90 minutes to eat our food in pubs, a photo appeared of an old man with an alarm clock beside his pint and dinner. It made international headlines, but it emerged days later that he just wanted to be home in time for the news.

The Man With The Clock

As if time was not precious enough
we have to chop it into little pieces
like a soggy wedding cake at 1am
to pass around, to make us feel
we have all had enough.
A tock to break the silence.
A tick to show the difference.
A grande sonnerie to break the hours
into four, so that when one ends,
another soon begins. A verge escapement
behind the face oiled to ease the melting
of one minute to another.
In my allotted time in public space.
My shot in the gaze of those
who normally look through me
until it suits them to stop
and see my space in theirs.

Being alive, not just a pulse or a flicker
behind a cornea. Sometimes there is life
but no living. So you respect this thing
like a new neighbour moved in beside ya.
You tip your cap to it and all it can do.
You give it respect, and you
find your quiet place where you can be
the mortal personification of your soul.

But for now, there is the soft satisfaction
of a bite washed down with a fine pint.
A "Ta síad ag teacht" for the age that's in it.
And a clock stopped to hold the world
from speeding the way it does.

Ireland had three Ministers for Agriculture last summer. Two resigned, before Micheal Martin took the role while he decided who should be the fourth holder of the office in a Government just a few months old.

The Fourth Minister

The Fourth Minister
has to keep the nose clean,
the head down,
the chin up
the best side out.
The Fourth Minister
has to be a Pioneer.
A real one.
Not one of those who
reject the drink for thirty years
and then turn into a mad hoor
after a weekend away
at a convention in Cavan.
The Fourth Minister has to wash his hands
before and after he uses the jacks.
Shower four times a day.
Not swear or click for MILFS on Google.
Not put in for an extra few miles
or that late takeaway at Applegreen.
The Fourth Minister has to look
at farm animals with total purity.
Has to wear wellies that don't look
like they were bought at Kildare Village yesterday.
The Fourth Minister has to be able to
calm a collie with a tickle around the ear.
To get to bed the same day he got up.
Get up the same day he went to bed.
The Fourth Minister has to make sure
not to order the stuffed avoca-do at the IFA-do.

But most of all, the Fourth Minister
has to not make a balls of it...
at least for a while and only then
for a good cause.

| 5 |
| 4.5 |
| 4+ |
| 4 |
| 3.75 |
| 3.5 |
| 3 |
| 3- |
| 2⁺ |

People say there were fewer storms in Ireland before we started labelling them and organising them into colours. Our lives are now governed by different statuses.

Finding your level

What happens if there's a Code Red storm
in a Level Three lockdown
with a Yellow Wind Warning?
Or if a lad with a big red N
on his car window meets
a girl with a H1 in Maths
during a Status Orange house party
in a Level Four setting?

What happens if the captain of
the Junior B team builds a house
just over the county border and
the day before the county final
the whole place moves up a step
and he has to stay at home and
watch the stream on dodgy broadband
that he got in for the working from home?

What happens if Rex from Texas
whose mother was Dunne from far-back
decides where to build his multimillion widget
factory based on how well a county fares
on the X Factor of the R Number?
"Hey, am I anywhere near Clane,"
He says to the auld lad on a tractor
who says "You're not, ya dirty JR Ewing fecker ya"

What happens if the CEO of the CAO
meets the CEO of the CSO
near the GPO and says that only those
who live in Level One or Two counties
can be trusted to go to college
and wash their hands to the tune of
a thousand Happy Birthdays while
holding a Sally Rooney novel
under their oxters?

Aw, lads,
As if life wasn't complicated enough.

Without real people dressing up as zombies in a cancelled Halloween, how would the real walking dead get around without being noticed?

The Solitary Souls of Samhain

'Twill be a hard year for the living dead.
The slow drag from the graveyard
as dripping dogs trail the scent of rotting flesh.
The Guards have no time for zombies
with their 'move along now, nawthing to see here lads'
not stirring the hollowed brains of the long passed.
While every year they hide among
the masks and grasps of those who mimic them,
now there is silence.
They stand alone on the main street
past the lines of vaping shops
of every town and village and wonder
where is everyone? Where are those who
smell of Paco and Coco
and not the belched returns of the fat worm?
The Hades bugler will not transmit that this time
the other side is fireside, huddled.
Bolstered by brandy and briquettes.
Fearing that which they normally celebrate.

For those freed from the brass buckled box,
their tattered shrouds will billow in the breeze
of an All Souls Night where the cloud
of memento mori stalks every threshold.
As the hooves of Donn's steed echo
off the cobbled streets of a frightened world,
he sets for home and awaits us there.
With the fake blood and the dead brides
of the vampires left dishonoured.

How often has the Irish flag being used by those proclaiming to be patriots while espousing poisonous policies?

The tattered flag

If the tattered flag was cut to shreds
and elastic-ed into a mask by an aged seamstress
with bits of old knickers and a wild streak,
there could be a conundrum for the patriots
who climb the other hill of every horizon we see.
And exhale at us their toxic creed.

Kerry and the country were thrust into sadness when it emerged that Fungie, the Dingle dolphin, had gone missing. But has he gone or just returned from whence he came?

When Fungie fecked off

Fungie knew what he was doing the morning he fecked off.
Out past the out beyond. Just before the dark sky was eaten
by a Pacman of a sun at his tail. Who knows where I'll go,
he told himself as he bounded, out where the waves rush high.
There are plenty more fish in the sea, rang the words
of his long passed mother as he went out and out and out.
You'll be grand, so you will. You've done your bit, now you're
called for active service at the court of Poseidon.
Lap up the love of Aphrodite and Apollo, be charged by
the power of their gaze and not the oohs and aaahs
of camera clad watchers forking out for a brief glimpse
of something grey against the greyer;
But this year, they did not come to pay homage.
Or will him into play. Maybe they had found
something else to distract them. Maybe it was time
to do something out of character.
So he followed the others, with their youthful energy.
Through the night they spun out
to where there was nothing but he and them.
In a year where many slip silently away
he has grasped the mantle to turn back
into the pirate from whence he came.

For a few weeks in autumn, every Monday brought news of a development on the vaccine front as companies boasted about their efficacy levels.

Needle Point

On a Monday morn.
Every Monday, they lay
down their coats
when the Dow bell rings.
Clear their throats
and proclaim
"I'll see your ninety
And raise ya
Ninety-five"
worth of Efficacy
and the hopes of
a world waiting for
the piercing of skin.

Gaping veins waiting to suck in that concoction
of nine tenths hope and one tenth patience.
The prayers to Askeplios answered. A Zoom call of
the Therapeutae of Asclepius unmuted.

A juxtaposition of worlds — The Oxford The Astra Zeneca the Moderna The Pfizer
like a list in a car-namers' hut in Dagenham. Like wheels, offering to change the world
for those who will rush to the docs and say 'put me down for all three;
and whatever you're having yourself, as soon as you can."

But haste not...

In Grand Designs, everyone
wants to be in by Christmas,
but waits until July when the
smell of builder's dust
leaves the nostrils
and the fatted finger runs clean
along the mantel of life.

When it emerged that Leo Varadkar had leaked documents to a friend, there was a political storm and the former Taoiseach had to apologise in Dáil Eireann

Leaks lip

When Tyrone was knocked
out of the All-Ireland on Sunday,
I didn't bat an eyelid because
on the Friday, Leo told me
what the result would be.
"What's your postal address,
my little non-rhyming Dutch friend?"
He says to me in a Whatsappy text
to the phone I don't have.

The lad from DHL arrived
all red and yellow-ed up on Tuesday
with Wednesday's Lotto numbers.
But when the visor went back
'twas the man himself.
"Leo always delivers," he says
throwing himself to the ground,
giving me fifty crunches,
grabbing my morning smoothie
and throwing
it all over himself.

"Tis Mary Lou's fault there's no
Dancing With The Stars next year.
But this is the lad who wins it," he said
showing me a piece of paper
and before I could tell him
there's just one L in Mescal,
he'd slipped me a vial of the vaccine
And was gone.

There's nothing wrong with
wanting everyone to love ya.

You just have to tell them all
one at a time.

As a restricted Ireland sat down to watch a virtual Late Late Toy Show,
our hearts were melted by a communal shared experience of soundness,
and weeping hearts for the bravery of our young.

Toy Show

Who would have thought
A country of rocks and winds
And hardened hoors would stall.
Just stop.
Dead. In its tracks.
On a drinking night
for a chat show where all guests
Are less than three feet tall.
I waited to see Mattel's finest
yet toys faded silently like the
mountain of teddy bears
in the background.
We heard the excited
voices of those
hopeful citizens
who never speak on TV after nine.

Into every sitting room,
falsetto tones rang out
past roaring fires
toasting furry jammies,
munching
Mr Tayto's latest work.
Stay-uppers
thrilled to see the clock
strike ten, eleven, twelve.
They tuned in for treats
but were taught a lesson
in how a country treats
its youngest. A Masters Degree in
soundness and decency
passed subliminally
with the crunch of crisps
into their voracious minds.

We all wept at bravery
and hope of those who
will walk this land after us,
who will lie in the shadows
of the trees we plant, and learn
kindness from that
shown to them
And others.

With no epidemiologist
in sight, we saw
what living with Covid means.
to the fun-size thinkers
who gave up the most this year.

In the week when the Galway International Arts Festival was meant to start, I wrote of missing out on the real deal.

Embracing Nothingness

Montepulciano is a bit manky
when the corners of the cream cracker
drop into it like ripped Acupulco divers.
Crack-ed not cork-ed.
Airkisses just look perverse
in the mirror and no matter
how much you tell yourself
you loved your play, the critic
at the back of your mind is
click clacking away a massacre
on the QUERTY of the old
typewriter. When all you meet
is yourself coming back from
the bathroom and your tweed
jacket and polo seem excessive
In the sitting room heat,
you know you can't replace
those late summer nights
when the thump thump thump
from that blue canvas
hops the river and gives
hangovers to lazy seagulls
picking the bones of long dead snackboxes.
The beautiful fake authenticity
of it all. A city ripped of its
juxtaposition
of Beckett and betting slips.
A JCB flattening the hill
of the high moral ground
to make way for a road
that brings nobody
from nowhere
to nothing.

As news emerged that the new vaccines would require specialised refrigerator space, we spared a thought for the discommoded frozen food that would have to make way.

Last few choc ices

Anyone for the last few Choc Ices
or Wibbly Wobbly Wonders
because they'll be discommoded
bigly when the vaccine arrives
and like the cuckoo, kicks them out
of their ice-covered nest.

There won't be a half empty packet
of soggy fish fingers left as every
fridge and freezer worth its weight
in frozen peas rents out its Baltic bedroom
to the blow-ins from Astra Zeneca
and Pfizer, sidling up to the Icebergers
and saying "move over in the bed there will ya?
For feck's sake, I need to be freeeeeeeeezzzin."

The delicate pastried tempura prawns,
the once a year festive spring rolls
and the Christmas hors-oeuvres,
which Seamus once thought
were really horses' ovaries,
wonderin' who the hell are these to be
coming in here, throwing shapes
like the time the Magnums
arrived and bullied the Brunches.

Let the vaccines not be sweating
about not being cold enough
here in the west of Ireland.
Let them with their fancy European ways
walk down a main street
in Belmullet on a damp December day
with the nose-drippings frozen
and dare to say they're too hot.
And when they've done their job,
next summer, we'll use the spare
fridges to cool down our long-trodden
excitement of this new world.

The great silverware of the Irish Gaelic Games season was to be handed out in empty stadiums on dark bleak weekend evenings in atmospheres that nobody had seen before or wanted to see again.

Winter champions

There'll be a glint of silver
in the darkness.
A stifled cheer suppressing
a lung-built roar.
Softness, like a sliotar cushioned
by a mossy turf,
damp from the dew of an Irish winter.
A saturated glove grasping
at elusive stitching.
A muffled honk
over a quiet sobbing
of joy and pride.
The nice rattle of a trophy
in a bag in the boot.
passing tinselled villages
to the captain's house.
A hidden solar gemstone
beating in the heart of its
hard-won community.
Wrapped, lest sight of it
will spark a sea of hugs.

There will be other days again
when the sun will shine
on speckled sweat.
Victors or not, those
who now fight for silver
are all winter champions.
Pushing blood through our veins,
Warming us, far from the
cold stand, shortening
the days,
like an equinox
on demand.

The prospect of coming home for Christmas and having to spend it isolated in your own teenage bedroom, proved a step too far for many emigrants this festive season.

Ovah

When Jimmy normally comes back from Ealing for the Christmas, he does so in a Beamer
he hires at Holyhead, and drives the hole off it across Ireland to let the lads know
how well he is doing ovah. "I'm doing good ovah. Me Flyin' it. Me."
He says flashing the Queen's money and saying he's a hundred men under him
and when he goes to the jacks to strain the spuds, the lads laugh at him
and say if he has, he must be grasscutting at Highgate cemetery.

Jimmy doesn't want to ate his dinner on a tray in the room he left Ireland
to get away from. To be talking through the door at those too deaf to hear him.
Too needy to be serving him. There are too many memories in that room.
A Bullworker that gave him strong arms. A creased Woman's Way picture of Bo Derek in 10
in the top drawer inside a Family Album catalogue mouldy from the dust.
A school jumper still folded in the drawer smelling of camphor balls and cobwebs.
A pair of desert boots. A team photo of lads half of whom are on their second marriage or second transplant.
A scattering of medals and plaques from back when he could see his toes without bending.

Comin' ovah wasn't on this year. Staying in his room with the auld pair
downstairs would be transporting him back to the ancient power struggles when he didn't know his arse from his elbow,
and he'd listen down through the bannisters to the groans of grownups,
borne from despair at being stuck in a town with not enough roads out of it, through suburbs where he'd burn his past
and take new papers like a witness protection scheme for the lost.

So this year Jimmy stayed away and ate his chicken dinner on a tray
in his own place overlooking frightened streets in a confused country blasting bullets at its toes and gnarling at its nose.
This, a year when all that thrilled him was no longer on offer.
The dousing of old flames, the rousing of aged jealousies, the strong horn for the going back.

The face looking back through the shaving foam and blunt Gillette
is more than a year older than it was this time last year.
"I'm not built for lockdown," he tells himself. No future, no past, no joy from ovah anymore.
Ovah here, ovah there, ovah and out.

In a summer of never-ending gloom, the rescue of two young Galway women whose surfboards drifted far out to sea lifted the hearts of us all.

The Rescue of Hope

(Tribute to the Olivers — Galway's sea heroes)

In the year when every flower wilted,
every puddle filled to spilling point,
every wind blew over what it could.
When the nightly roll-call of
the departed holders
of underlying conditions,
brought sorrow and heavy hearts to
our chests, we looked in vain
for an air of solace
and found none.

Until this week...

For hour after hour, we slept unknowing as
the cousins lay on beds of epoxy
and fibre glass
and created the tale
they will recall over plates of
peppery pasta
in the decades ahead.
They scanned the western sky and listened
as up the clinging rope came the nighttime tune
of the Lobster Quadrille
sang by crustaceans
also uncertain of their fate.

Together they looked at waters
oft miscast as Synge's son-stealers
while welcome waves lapped them
to the shore of self-belief.
That if they hoped enough
for long enough, the fresh faced saviours
who peered into their eyes would bring
home a tale to lift a nation,
To tell us there is hope
where we least expect it.

There was consternation when it was revealed that some councillors were looking to have their mileage allowance paid for travel to meetings, even though the meetings were held on Zoom.

Money For Muting and Your Chips for Free

Sheila knew there was method to Paddy's madness
when he asked for a measuring tape for Christmas
and found him on his knees counting the inches
from the kitchen to the front room where the convoluted
Dell laptop the council gave him, sat on the coffee table beside the
book with all the former black and white pictures
that he gave her on Christmas morning.
Not saying that he got it free with the drink
from the lad in the quarry who was very grateful
for the new access road through where the rare squirrels lived.
"Mattie," she heard him roar down to the phone.
"If I charge da mileage by making the inches miles, am I quids in?"
"Naw, ya gob shyatttt, make the centimetres miles,
and ya'll do better," she heard his colleague on
The Council Sheep Dipping Commitee roar down the line at him.
"Ya can say da figures were lost in translation like. They'll
not be mane spirited 'bout it this year of all years.
"Never mind da Lavin' Cert and the odd weddin'
and funerals we can't go ta. But what about us like?
Cos we have still ta do the tinkin'.
To ask d'experts the questions.
To do the advo catin'.
They have ta fork out for our inta-lectual property like.
"D'only raisin I did this was for da mileage. Long journeys
to the arsehoooole of Donegal for the Health Forum matin'
And long journeys back with a stop each way for a no-receipt needed bite
to ate
cos ya can't be doing this for da love of it.
When ya had a Council matin' in the town, they gave ya
chocolate goldgrain and Kimberley's biskits and ya got
ta drop the kids to college but now, if I want
a cuppa tay or a plate of chips,
then I've ta git it and pay for it meself."
"Dat auld Zoom ting gives ya the treble chins too, so
I'm getting paid no money for getting fatter
and for every wan commentin' on me shite wallpaper
and the press full of dusty Encyclopaedia Britannica that
we bought from some flute in 1991
But which have never been opened.
"Ya have to be smart about it, Paddy. Lash in a load of
questions at the start of the matin', make them sick
o' your face, then mute the camera and all.
And head off down the farm til the cows come home
And feck the begrudgers."

As vaccines started to be handed out to GP surgeries around the country, the over 85s waited by the telephone for the call from their doctor with details of their long awaited vaccination.

Hanging on the telephone

Mary told the sisters not to be ringing her with news of who's dead
and who's dying and that the cousin in Coventry got done four weeks ago
but then why wouldn't she 'cos her kids aren't wasters and they knew
someone who knew someone and they've the big job with the letters after their names
And....although we didn't have cougars in the 1950s, the fact that Maggie Tuohy
married the lad seven years younger than her in 1962 means they'll get the jab two months
apart which will soften their cough and slow down their gallivanting to tea dances
and get togethers where they jive like young ones making a holy show of themselves.

"Get off the line," says Mary when she gets the chance to stick a word in edgeways
'Cos the doctor could be calling to give me the time for the jab.
My one shot at redemption, my key to get out to grab my life back
My day pass for good behaviour. My release from the closed open prison of my home.
A scarce year wasted while I waited for science to catch up with my impatience.
'Tis ok for the younger ones to be talking about it being just another year.
But while years are just like ripples in the rockpool to them, to me they are waves.
Slowly ebbing against the rocks, but fast enough for me to count them and know
their limitations. That soon the wet sand gets drier and drier.
"Old lives matter," she says to the sister. "I'd get up at four in the morning to get this.
To feel alive again, to be a part of what I created and not just a thing to be minded.

When the first vaccines arrived, it emerged that some people were given it. Sons and daughters of the privileged and people who were not on the first priority list.

Draining the dregs

Come on in here out of the garden. Lay down the spades and shovels and roll up that sleeve while we wait for the young lad to finish his round and get here from the club. Go get your mother and stay mum for the shot. Climb down from the scaffold. There'll be no wasting a drop of this stuff. Not a drop
We'll drain the dregs. Twelve doses a go. Pore through the contacts book. Get here before it goes mouldy. Queueing is for the little people. Let Darby O'Gill get to the back of the line because because. Fret not about the optics. A ship passing in the night. A rushed apology on headed paper will quell the unrest. A sorry me hole for those who cannot believe that they would ever see anything wrong with it. We didn't want it to go to waste, so the hospital cat, and the pigeons who coo on the roofs were dragged in, paws and wings lifted and given the dose, because ya don't want it to go to waste. So fuck the begrudgers. Let those who watch over gasping last breaths with elastic burning into the former softness of their face await the natural order. Come the summer, there'll be giving these out with snackboxes and choc ices across the fairgrounds and pitches of Ireland. They'll be this year's bread and toilet rolls. Something we forgot we ever wanted. There'll be little phials in the bottom of cereal boxes. A one for everyone in the audience. Something you get with a fill of diesel and a coffee. And in the summer of our bounce back, we'll return to the land of the shift and the salt and vinegar-flavoured grope of the lost intimacies of a celibate country deprived. A nation roused by the fleshfests of Normal People, Bridgerton and Operation Transformation. When nobody will give a damn about who got what and when and who did what and with what to whom. We'll not have wasted a drop. Not a drop.

When it emerged that people were breaking their 5km rule to travel to Dublin Airport to fly to sunspots like Lanzarote and Tenerife, there was outcry in the country.

Stay Out, Ye Back and Tanned

If Jimmy with his newly-tanned arse slips
on the ice and ends up in casualty next week
and has to look into the reddened eyes
and mask-scarred faces of those who held
the frightened hands of the dying, let him
feel the searing shame of letting down those
he'll need to save him.
If Geraldine has to extol the virtues of the latest bronzer
to those who wink and whisper
"Jaysis Ger you've a grand colour'
and they knowing damn well that her car
wasn't outside the house for the past ten days,
let the dark grains of sand still rattling around her Converse
remind her of the ashes of the early departed.

Let the ringing songs of sunshine karaoke echo
round their heads and drown out the drawing wheeze
as the claws of this bastard virus scrape down
the lungs of those not ready to go. Let's hope
the timid heat of the January sun
was worth the treacherous fuck you
to the gowned and tired nurses,
crawling home at dawn after a night of caressing death.
Stripping down in sheds lest they infect their own.

I'd love to know what part of you was above all this.
You, not feeling the fear that feeds the feeble,
shuffling behind the net curtain looking out at a forbidden
world that has found a new way to kill them

All because you wanted a tan that nobody can see.

The whole world stayed up to see how America voted in November, with particular focus on Florida.

The swing state of them

"America is a great country for the upholstery,"
said Seamus to me this morning. "These feckers
in Florida were mostly born before 1950 but are
made up of materials made in Westport."

"If it wasn't for the Irish botox, half of Florida
would look like we do." he said. "Worn down by life
with teeth like dolmens and chins that are
nearer our arse than our head.

"They've the great big Kennedy hair
and the great big Kennedy teeth
'cos they had the fluoride and the conditioner
way before we had toothpaste.

"But they're held together by the glue
of the labs of the world, so they've serious
skin in the game of science. They're
showing they're in no hurry to go anywhere.

"And tonight, we'll wait up half the night
to see how decisions they make
shape the state of the world for the
next four years," he said.

And by then or Biden,
science might have found more ways
to ensure they get a vote
the next time around.

At the heart of Government, we have a man who knows everything and is able to tell us that, whether he does know everything or not.

The Man Who Knows Everything

The Man Who Knows Everything
Enunciates...
Spells it out.
Says it slowly.
Drags every last bit out of it.
Breaks it down
so that even the
most utter and complete
gobshite among us
will know that
The Man Who Knows Everything
thinks we know nawthing
and is doing us a favour
by letting us drink from his
vast goblet of knowledge.

The Man Who Knows Everything
knows it
Just five minutes
before we do,
yet we must listen
as if it is the stuff of ages.

The Man Who Knows Everything
was once The Lad Who Knew Something
But Thought He Knew Everything.
Yet now he has the keys
to new original material
and so we wait with
open beaks to hear
His latest take
on our fragile fate.

When it was reported that President Trump had referred to the fallen soldiers as 'suckers and losers,' it caused upset among the families of the heroes.

Last Revenge of the Suckers and Losers

By cocking an eye in
the rear view mirror of history,
do we know
where we go.
Only by dragging your mind
through the muddy ditches browned
with the long dried blood of suckers and losers,
can we know who we are
and who we are not.

All our fate has been shaped by the shivering
bravery of the suckers and losers. All our hopes created
by those who ask not why or how much
But every day fill their hands with the work felt by many.

If the disdain of the despicable for these suckers and losers
is what rids the world of the stain He has spilt
upon the blue canvas, it will be a good day's work
for those who stand on the wall
as we rest our heads.

I wondered why in many Irish political scandals such as Bertie in Manchester, the Broadband saga, and Golfgate, that the need to 'eat a dinner' is at the forefront. What is this Irish obsession for 'the spuds?'

'Tis the dinner that ruins us

Tis always stayin' for the dinner that
ruins us. Destroys our thinking. If we
hadn't the same harking for
a few spuds, carrots that look
like they've been chewed already
or a glance through
sirloin eyes, there'd be more
sympathy for the lads in the muck.

There are those who are less guilty;
Freed from public opprobrium;
Granted non conditional immunity because
when the full judicial review was published,
it was determined that 'twas the liking for the balls of mash
and the lashings of gravy that swayed the mind.

They say you can't be dodgy if you've sat for the dinner.
You've committed yourself to the whole hog.
Starter of melon or soup. The beef or the salmon.
The chocolate profiteroles with their skid marks
across the finest Wedgewood. And even the
After Eight with the Bewleys to wash it down.

If you're up to no good, you don't have time for the dinner.
You sit in the bar, keep notes, sip a coffee, leave the car running
for the quick getaway. Here, to find the guilty parties,
You follow the spuds and the trail of Bisto.

In a year when we needed them more than ever, our artists and singers and creatives were left without audiences. Particularly in Galway which had been impacted more than most because of the decimation of the Galway 2020 programme.

The Thief Who Stole Our Culture

Above all years, above all times
we could not afford the thief
stealing the gaze from the artist,
robbing her of what makes her heart beat.
The cad who took a scissors
To snip the vocal chords of those
who sing like larks.
The divil who smashed the mirror of joviality
That feeds our comedians
And emboldens them for the next line.
What would sweet Carolan have thought
If only the birds had an audience to warble to.

In a year when we lifted the cobbles and
replaced them with dull flat
hot tar to throw at the remaining buskers
whose stage left is a side street.
When the wind and rain soiled everything.
When we naively thought we could create
an iconic image of ourselves by
unloading a truckload of Ireland from
somewhere east of Holyhead.
Something that worked somewhere else.
Not ours. But a hand me down
From the Emperor's wardrobe.

At a time when vast hordes got the
ride off lustful Angst, let us drop worms into
the beaks of those who conduct the
pictorial soundtrack of a life worth living.
Let the voice of the poet ring free
to tell the world what has happened.
This creative army cannot march
on empty stomachs. Without them
there is nowhere for us to truly see ourselves.

A clock stopped on a million years
of attuned ears acting as custodians.
A break unscheduled.
Must the harpists of the Earls
Once again go hungry before they
dine heartily at the table of appreciation?

Mind the gap.
We hear a lot about a future where we live with Covid, but what if we like
our own company?

Co-habiting with Covid

Sometimes there is living
when you are dead inside.
Maybe breathing is over-rated.
Life is not just a pulse or a flicker
behind a cornea. Moving more
than just a battle against rigor mortis.

As if time wasn't precious
or scarce enough. Every summer
a lament to those gone,
not those coming.
Every autumn a prelude
to a Christmas which could be your last.

The power to dream technicolour
turned to monochrome
Every possibility shattered,
now I must live with a new flatmate.
One that I shunned. One who holds
all night parties in your head.
If Covid is a tenant, we must talk to it, engage.
What is this tenancy if you fear what you live with
is the Single White Female of illnesses.
Waiting around every corner
To catch you unawares.

The news that the commission into the Mother and Baby Homes may have deleted the audio recordings of those who gave hard-delivered evidence caused great shock. Later, it was reported that a back up copy was available. But it should never have come to that stage.

Gone

Did they write this report with their coats on?
One ear cocked for the last bus, the other half listening
yeah yeah yeah to the strangled tears of the unheard,
unburdening stories of dark nights where the hard leather of the sisters' shoes
rat-a-tatted down cold parqueted corridors to Fedex a putdown
or a haunting slapped thought that couldn't wait 'til morning.
So when they got the chance, the pale stunned spewed out
tales of fear and loathing they thought might remain buried in the damp yard
of a black and white world where nothing good ever happened.

When the lad in RTE left the plastic clips on the top of the video-cassette
and let it all record over those first years of Wanderley Wagon,
we knew we had a problem in minding stuff we should keep.

And with a button, it was gone.
What took decades to recall, a treasure trove of the sort of horrid memories
a country needs to improve itself; cast aside and deemed a worthless insult
by the academics and legals who never knew the lash of a stick
or the back of a hand in a place where no-one heard you scream.

If we wanted to flush our faux sincerity through the septic tanks of Tuam;
To bask as smirking torchholders aiming lumens into oft quoted dark corners;
To stand on the little skulls and crush them into dust;
To spit in the faces of those who had to learn to talk again after our State's agents
bate the love of life out of them; we could not do much more
than fling their hard-told stories into that dark place
that even now tonight hums with the drip of foul wastewater and tears,
beating out a backing track to the groans of the long departed.

What would they know, these women with their talking to each other
and sharing stories — As if they had to conspire to imagine horrors imposed.
As if the nuns and councils never put their heads together.
Dark suits and veils, a marriage of hair grease and soft talc
on the nodding skulls of the see-no-evils.
It wasn't enough for those long dead to call them names.
Now we deem them untrustworthy liars, whose words don't even deserve to be kept.

'Tis easy to bin a pdf, especially one ten times longer than the longest novel.
This body-less thing a symbol of the c'mon to fuck-ness haste which said
'yeah you're grand, thanks for sharing your sad life
but sure we don't believe a word of it, so off with ya now.
You with your fear-scarred visage and your trampled hearts.
I've the leafy suburbs to get back to and the Times to read.

There was a lot of focus on the idea of the 'substantial meal' for €9 and how diners would prove that they were eating and not just skulling pints.

Larry had Lasagne

There on the screen in big letters on
whatdidyoureallyate.ie was the evidence
that Larry had lasagne that day in the pub.
With chips
And mash
And a bit of that Pilau rice 'for the health like.'
Granny had the half portion 'cos she
isn't able to chew a full chicken breast
in 90 minutes though Larry told her that
half portion doesn't mean half price
and that he'd ate the other half
if she went for the full one.
Grandad ordered some nondescript
fishy thing he didn't fancy saying
What da feck is beeeeeeesk,
but which Granny might like if
she wasn't gone on the half chicken
and asked him to swap.

And while they munched their meals
an algorithm drawn up by a teen
atin' a burrito and fries
was sending Granny's details to
a computer deep in the bowels
of Fianna Fáil HQ
And because of that spoon-een
of pilau, Larry would be getting emails
from the Greens.

Grandad was marked a Don't Know.

In August, Storm Ellen was, before hitting Ireland, classified as a so-called "weather bomb" or bomb cyclone. So we sat and waited through a long night.

For Ellen

I shut my eyes and
let the tap tap tap of the ivy
outside my window
beat out a message from
the wind that lapped at
Moher moments ago.

Huddle in your beds
you mere mortal man.
Shrink from my arms
that could fling you
across Inagh.
I am not a teatime
directive signed and
delivered on
a skinny podium.
Nor am I a guideline.
I can stop your
gallivanting
with a twist this way
or that.
You will not know 'til
dawn what havoc
I wreak, so sleep now.
Let me do my worst
to the fattened crann
that fawns before me.

And at my hour,
I will be done.

My childhood friend Dirk de Vries draws the little images for this book. One night last year, we spent drinking red wine, talking our country's football hopes and doodling.

Dirk the Doodler

He swears as a glob
of red wine splashes
onto paper just missing
what is supposed to be
my face... a squiggle of
split ends and a brow
lined by the ploughman
of life.

'You've gotten old, ya bastard'
he growls at me. 'There was a
time when you needed fewer lines
than now. My strokes were broad.
Your head a globe searching its
place in the universe.
But now, it's a canyon.
Peaks and troughs of
skin creased by thoughts of
the next good day.

"But it's the eyes. They still have
that sparkle of university," he says

His hands still mystify me
A magician's wand with
Every swivel, still the young
man who made them swoon
back then when life
was full of Cruyff and Rep
and Neeskens and Sylvia Kristel.

He tosses over the sheet
And laughs as a stream
of Montepulciano
Gives me a moving bandana.

Nobody was sad to see the end of 2020, and New Year's Eve was a muted affair for everyone.

The bad cess

Mary shed a tear when her tea went cold
on the table set for one in front of the telly,
as the leader walked down those steps.
Be sensible and careful, she heard him say.
Bheith ciallmhar agus cúramach.
And she nothing but, in the months
since she became One. Since her beloved
Frank was carried by her nephews
around the bend from the livingroom into the hall.
Out through the door that for every year
of their union, they opened as St Nicholas' bell
struck midnight to let out the bad cess
of the year just gone and embrace
the freshness of a new tomorrow.
Each time chilled by the frost of a hairy moon
bouncing off the bay in the
stillness of a New Year's `Night.
Each time, warmed by the hug
He gave her as they shut out the night.
She can still feel the press of the last one.
Weaker than the others.

She knows she'll soon get the call from the doc
for the chance to stave off the time
when she'll be with Frank again.
She hasn't stepped in there
since the day she got the cert that told of
his loving and his leaving.

Tonight, she'll lean alone against the frame
and look out over a quiet Galway
lit up by a rogue firework, hear the rare roar
from afar and inhale the night air missing
the loving touch of the city chimes.

And then she'll shove over that bolt
that keeps out everything but time
And pray herself into the morn of a New Year.

As we struggled to come to terms with the winter/spring lockdown,
we wondered about the price we paid for having had a
'meaningful Christmas.'

A meaningful Pancake Tuesday

When we've strained the last bit of Heaney
out of the works and we've stopped trying
to decipher what bollocks is in sign language.
If we stop the drinking' and the ridin'
and the horsin' in through hotel windows
to get to the spilt tears of another lost All-Ireland.
If we stop trying to kill the teachers and
deny their hot summers working in Boston.
If we can make the Leaving Cert students
forget what they're supposed to be remembering
to rhyme off over ten sweaty days in June.
If we can stop trying to apologise to our new friends
for the Ursuline actions of our old friends.
If we can stop looking for answers in a report
where the tear-soaked replies were wiped out
by all three monkeys with fingers stuck in their ears.
If we can stop shouting about the kids of the master
batin' us to the top of the jab queue.
If we can build up the courage to foresee a future
where one day we can all climb back up on our trampolines
And bounce our way through Terminal 2 to rid our pallid visage
of the porcelain look that branded our previous poverty.

I was commissioned to write this poem in honour of the tremendous work undertaken by the members of the Galway Volunteer Centre.

'Tis only me

(For Galway Volunteer Centre)

There's a biting point that snaps
when the honest truth of giving,
locks into place with the humbled gratitude
of the waiting one who hears
the soft footsteps on the path.
The cheerful push of the bell;
the nestled rustle of the bags for life
leaning against the door
as a "tis only me" echoes through the coloured glass
and down the hallway.

And when that door snaps shut and shy farewells are passed,
the net curtain is moved aside to verify
the corporeal wholeness of those
who care enough to let them know they matter.
You all, a vast local grid of human energy
eschew the draw of Netflix and Deliveroo
to answer a call of humanity from within.
You let the couch cushions fill out.
Your chests swell with the fulfilment
of making a real difference.

A telepathic message which powers you
to create a massive light to those
who feel the world has darkened.
Thousands will see a summer sun
because of winter warmth
stoked by your selflessness.
They are insulated by your real goodness.
That you have become the person
your mother wanted you to be.
That your precious time,
shared in this collective cloud of soundness,
will stir a daily dawn of hope.

For those whose well of love and dignity has dried,
You come, all collars raised against the stern wind
with pails of care and love.
So that at night as their blanket is pulled
up to their nose, they smile at the big sky that lights your way.
As you wake, they wake and thank the world that you exist.
For gracing you the energy to take interest in their lives.

Your place has become a better land
because you fill the cracks of need, make the invisible visible,
spark the hardened face into a smile of spring.
Not a dog left unwalked. Not a chat left unsaid,
you pump love through the arteries of a community
And make it strong.
You might think 'tis only me
How glad are we that 'tis only you?
Our heroes who give your all to all.

Father Eddie doesn't do telly anymore

Father Eddie never thought he'd be rated anymore.
By anyone outside the Curia that is;
or the Diocesan secretary;
or the woman who insisted on holding lockdown Rosary at the grotto
while flaunting the rules of social distancing
and told him to fuck off with himself
while fingering the beads in her hand.

They say he once made films in Biafra, took pictures for the Far East
magazine.
His fresh face in the black and white of a Radharc (Rye Ark)
documentary about a new water pump for a village.
A 16 mill sync-sound camera on his arm
on a street with hundreds of locals alongside, eyes open
in wonder. His hair a rich black against his bright linen suit
in the unrelenting heat of a Kenyan day.

He thought he could fade now, disappear gracefully
into the long night of the rural Irish parish.
To be buried 'neath a tree in the churchyard.
Instead, his calloused hands mop his brow
and struggle with the fidgety buttons
on the newfangled Youtube camera
up there where the choir used to sing.

Now they comment on him, his look, his sound,
the ones who you thought would never bother
logging in on a Sunday morning,
The pass-remarkable without mothers to chide them
for not going to Mass and listening to what was being said.
They mock his modern day Carraig an Aifrinn;
his slow ways; the way he racks his minds for the words
that once fell easy onto open ears.

He stares down the aisle at the red light,
his soft voice echoing off the emptiness, bouncing to
the lens that carries his word out
to the 48 or so who logged in last week.
He nods a thanks to the man and woman who
stand at the locked door in high vis,
ready to spray Dettol on everything
he's touched. As soon as he's back in the
sanctuary of the sacristy, he thanks the Lord
and switches off the world for another week.

The controversy over an image of Gordon Elliott sitting astride a dead horse caused much outrage in March.

The Horse Who Sat On The Dead Man

We love all men, so we do, said the horse
the morning after the image appeared of a stallion
straddling a dead man. Mane flung back and he laughing his hole off
with the other horses. Like as if dissing the dead man was something the
horses did every day.
Which it's not. Of course. Nothing could be further
from the truth, said the horse. In all seriousness.
"It's not fair that you're judging all horses for this," he said.
"Twas a moment of madness. We've great time for men, haven't we lads?
says he to the other horses nodding at the side of the gallops.
"I was just walking by and the man went Boom.
Falling like one of George Lee's flies on the nine o'clock news.
Lights out, Kaputt. Fecked. Gone to meet the maker. Bollocks-ed.
And ya know how it is with hearses these days and undertakers
And you're waiting for them because they're so busy running hardware
stores
and delivering briquettes before the bog runs out of them
that it takes a while for them to get here.
So the dead man's going nowhere.
So I just think to meself, that maybe, while I'm waiting there, standing
twenty hands high behind him that there'd be nothing wrong with
Me sitting down on him, like a sign of affection or something.
For old time's sake. Or in case the wind might come and blow him away,
to act like a sort of paper weight. And when the shit hit the fan
back in the stables, all the horses who liked men said
they'd have nothing to do with the stallion anymore
Because after all, what's to say that all stallions
aren't sitting on dead men everywhere everyday.
And to placate the men, (the live ones) the horses said they wanted the
stallion
to pay the price for his moment of madness.
and suggested that the horse should become a donkey. An asal.
For a year. Well maybe not a year, 'cos a year is a long time.
So maybe half a year, cos as we all know half a year is only about
two weeks in a horse life.
And the horses who defended the horses hang their long faces in shame
Saying 'twas terrible he got caught 'cos there's no telling where cameras
will be nowadays.

And so to the end of this second collection. It finds us all at a crossroads, with many roads leading west to the setting sun and the glow of hope.

To Be Among

I want my rough visage to feel the warm heat of a world
that doesn't shirk from the kiss of an orange sunset.
Its soft shadows moving past crevices
of lived-in faces kept pale by the fear of
that nightly roll-call of the dead,
back when living by numbers shaped our mood.
I long for the lapping tongue of freedom
to cool my brow, to comfort minds set ablaze
by the night terrors of days without names.
When each dawn would see me forgot where and when and why.
Peering out through restful curtains at infant light
creeping over empty streets.
I want to sit now, legs akimbo around a small table
and feel the faint heat of a soft bun, the ebbing tide of cafe coffee
served in a cup resting against the bristles on my chin.
The hum of recognition above the colliding crash of delph.
I want to see green swathes trampled by young feet
extolling the names of heroes from global battles.
To see them sweat, exhausted, covered
with the earnest dry dust of summer.
I want the spirit of Gaillimh iníon Breasail
To rise from the waters than split us.
To stand on the rock that failed her and oversee
a new time of love for life.
I want to smell the grapes of the red while
oiled crumbs fall into my lap.
I want to wake into an order again; and not be
a disciple to my own yearnings.
I want to have to be
in a place where others expect me.
To be among again, and not alone to squeeze
lusty black ink onto thirsty yellow pages.
To feel the gaze of bright eyes
on my back, as the sun rises on
the hour of the survivors.

I lift my eyes...and hope.

Printed in Great Britain
by Amazon